T0115524

I Love You,

ZooBorns!

by Andrew Bleiman and Chris Eastland

Most of the photos in this book were previously published in
ZooBorns: The Newest, Cutest Animals from the World's Zoos and Aquariums.

Ready-to-Read

Simon Spotlight

New York London Toronto Sydney New Delhi

SIMON SPOTLIGHT

An imprint of Simon & Schuster Children's Publishing Division

1230 Avenue of the Americas, New York, New York 10020

Text copyright © 2012 by ZooBorns LLC

Photos copyright © 2010, 2012 by ZooBorns LLC

Most of the photos in this book were previously published in *ZooBorns: The Newest, Cutest Animals from the World's Zoos and Aquariums*. All rights reserved, including the right of reproduction in whole or in part in any form.

SIMON SPOTLIGHT, READY-TO-READ, and colophon are registered trademarks of Simon & Schuster, Inc.

For information about special discounts for bulk purchases, please contact Simon & Schuster Special Sales at 1-866-506-1949 or business@simonandschuster.com.

The Simon & Schuster Speakers Bureau can bring authors to your live event. For more information or to book an event contact the Simon & Schuster Speakers Bureau at 1-866-248-3049 or visit our website at www.simonspeakers.com.

Manufactured in the United States of America 0712 LAK

First Edition

10 9 8 7 6 5 4 3 2 1

Library of Congress Cataloging-in-Publication Data

Bleiman, Andrew.

I love you, ZooBorns! / by Andrew Bleiman and Chris Eastland. — 1st ed.p. cm. — (Ready-to-read)

ISBN 978-1-4424-4380-8 (pbk. : alk. paper) — ISBN 978-1-4424-4379-2 (hardcover : alk. paper) —

ISBN 978-1-4424-4381-5 (ebook) 1. Zoo animals—Infancy—Juvenile literature. I. Eastland, Chris. II. Title. III. Title: I love you, Zoo Borns!

QL77.5.B5385 2012

590.73—dc23

2012008983

Welcome to the wonderful world of
ZooBorns!

The newborn animals featured in this book live
in zoos around the world. Get to know them through
adorable photos and fun facts written in language that
is just right for emerging readers. Your child might not
be able to pronounce all the animal species names yet,
but if you stay close by, you can help sound them out.

This book can also be used as a tool to begin a
conversation about endangered species. The more
we learn about animals in zoos, the more we can do
to protect animals in the wild. Please visit your
local accredited zoo or aquarium to learn more!

Good morning!
This giant panda is ready
to start his day.

I love you, baby panda!

It is bath time for
Prince Harry, the baby
pygmy hippo.
He loves to splash
in the water.

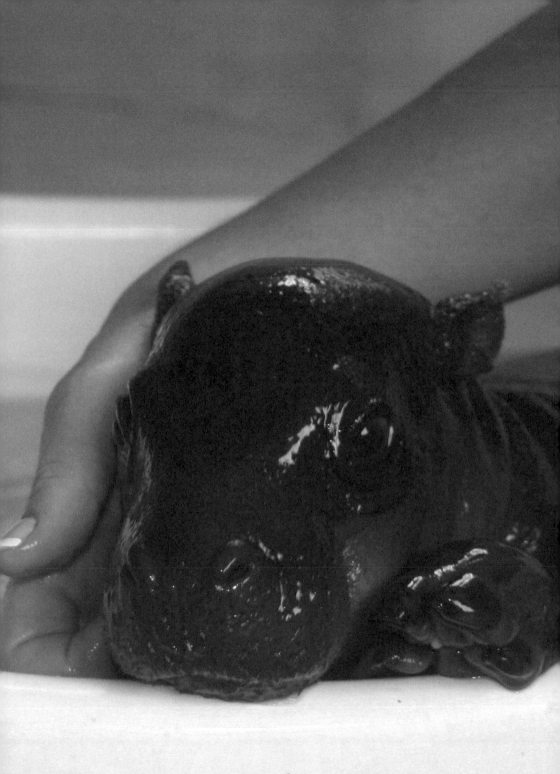

I love you, baby hippo!

Sawyer is a tawny frogmouth.
This bird loves to hop from one foot to the other.

I love you, baby frogmouth!

This common wombat loves lunchtime! But he sleeps during the day, so he eats lunch in the middle of the night.

I love you, baby wombat!

What do the baby
wildcats see?
They are all
very curious kitties!

I love you, baby wildcats!

Penguins love to waddle from place to place. They also love to slide across the ice to get to where they are going. This baby gentoo penguin is ready to slide.

I love you, baby penguin!

Lucy, the emperor tamarin, loves being brushed. She is so small that the zookeeper uses a toothbrush!

I love you, baby tamarin!

When these otter pups are awake, they are very noisy. They love to chirp.

Right now, they are snuggling
in a big pile.
I love you, baby otters!

Tahina, the crowned
sifaka lemur, is very tiny.

She loves to hug
her big stuffed teddy bear.
I love you, baby lemur!

Rooby, the red kangaroo, loves being wrapped up in a warm blanket. It feels just like she is in her mom's pouch!

I love you, baby kangaroo!

Special thanks to the photographers and institutions that made ZooBorns! possible:

Cover:
VANCOUVER ISLAND MARMOT
John Ternan/Calgary Zoo

GIANT PANDA
Yun Zi
Zoological Society of San Diego

GENTOO PENGUIN
Bob Couey/SeaWorld San Diego

PYGMY HIPPOPOTAMUS
Prince Harry
Tammy Moult/Cango Wildlife Ranch

EMPEROR TAMARIN
Lucy
Dave Parsons/Denver Zoo

TAWNY FROGMOUTH
Sawyer
Jason Collier/SeaWorld, Orlando

ASIAN SMALL-CLAWED OTTERS
Jason Collier/SeaWorld Orlando

COMMON WOMBAT
Matari
Lorinda Taylor/Taronga Zoo

CROWNED SIFAKA
Tahina
Musée de Besançon

WILDCATS
Joachim S. Muller taken at Opel Zoo

RED KANGAROO
Rooby
Darlene Stack/Assiniboine Park Zoo